JOSEP M. BENET I JORNET
LEGACY
Translated by **JANET DECESARIS**
ESTRENO Contemporary Spanish Plays 17

ESTRENO Collection of Contemporary Spanish Plays

General Editor: Phyllis Zatlin

LEGACY

JOSEP M. BENET I JORNET

LEGACY

(Testament)

Translation from the Catalan

by

Janet DeCesaris

ESTRENO Plays
New Brunswick, New Jersey
2000

ESTRENO Contemporary Spanish Plays 17
General Editor: Phyllis Zatlin
   Department of Spanish & Portuguese
   Faculty of Arts & Sciences
   Rutgers, The State University of New Jersey
   105 George Street
   New Brunswick, NJ 08901-1414 USA

Library of Congress Cataloging-in-Publication Data
Benet i Jornet, Josep Maria, 1940
   Legacy
   Translation of: Testament
   Contents: Legacy.
   1. Benet i Jornet, Josep Maria, 1940 Translation, English.
   I. DeCesaris, Janet. II. Title
Library of Congress Catalog Card No.: 99-71172
ISBN: 1-888463-09-0

© 2000 Copyright by ESTRENO Plays

Original Play © Josep M. Benet i Jornet, 1996.
English Translation © Janet DeCesaris, 2000
First Edition

All rights reserved.

Except for brief passages quoted in newspapers, magazines, radio or television, no part of this publication may be reproduced or transmitted in any form or by any means, electronic or mechanical, including photocopy, recording, or by an information storage and retrieval system, without permission in writing from the publisher.

Published with support from
Institució de les Lletres Catalanes

Cover: Jeffrey Eads

A NOTE ON THE PLAY

Those who expect to find exoticism, or at least foreignness in a play written in Catalan--a language that was under threat of extinction until recently, but kept alive by a separatist minority in Spain and France--must look elsewhere. *Testamen*by Josep M. Benet i Jornet strives for contemporary universality and finds it effortlessly. This is achieved not only because of the commonality of changing social mores and the trappings of technology across our contemporary world, but by a concerted effort to strip away any superfluous detail that may distract from its central human drama and the carefully honed complexity of its characters.

If one describes its central conflict in a succinct way, the wrong expectations are raised again. An aging man, a visiting lecturer at his old alma mater, develops an obsessive infatuation for an ostensibly heterosexual male student who turns out to use prostitution to support himself. A plot like this in the wrong hands would take us to the maudlin world of daytime talk shows. In this case, however, there is not even the hint of melodrama. Exploitation of human suffering, gender politics and the culture of victimization are totally absent.

In its place, we have a formalist series of concentric circles, rippling like waves in the placid lake of academia. At the center of this closed universe are the professor and the student. The next closed circle includes the professor's best friend from his youth, another male professor who has a tenured position at the same university. This circle expands to include the friend's family. The friend's daughter is pregnant by the same male student, who refuses to assume any responsibility. The young woman is debating whether to have the child or seek an abortion.

Rather than focusing on the sordid aspects of this tragic dilemma, the play shifts its focus to the academic pursuits of the visiting professor. The subject of his course is a medieval Catalan writer, Raymond Lully (Ramon Llull), immersed in Christian mysticism and alchemy. Lully's possible legacy to a contemporary mind becomes the metaphysical core of this play, as the professor tries in vain to pass his knowledge of this obscure thinker to the student, in an effort to transcend his imminent death from an incurable disease and leave a legacy to this young man that in some way he wishes was not his heir, but the son he never had. One could speculate whether one could substitute for Lully a writer less obscure to an English-speaking audience, perhaps William Blake. In fact, for all of the author's attempts at universality, when it comes to Lully, no substitute would do. This is why *Legacy* is firmly rooted in Catalan culture and can be translated, but not transposed.

Not content with giving us a simple drama, Benet i Jornet surrounds his central characters with a chorus of anonymous voices, heard in snatches of telephone conversations at the beginning of the play, during scene transitions, and at the end. The closed universe of the central characters is burst open to infinity by this device. Our need for a completed narrative is constantly disrupted by these fragments of human drama, devoid of identity. It is in this chorus of echoes that *Legacy* achieves its most resonant impact.

Lorenzo Mans
Literary Manager
INTAR Hispanic American Arts Center

ABOUT THE PLAYWRIGHT

Born in Barcelona in 1940, Josep Maria Benet i Jornet is by far the most popular playwright in Catalonia today. A frequent guest on Catalan public television, he is noted for his charming and open personality. Moreover, his soap opera scripts for Catalan television (four major series since 1994) have made him a celebrity.

Although Benet i Jornet prefers to consider himself a playwright rather than a scriptwriter, he does not deny that his soap operas may have contributed to the current flourishing of Catalan theatre. General interest for theatre rises as spectators flock to see the soap opera actors perform on stage. As a result, contemporary theatre of ideas is reaching mainstream audiences. For example, in 1999, Benet's *El Gos del Tinent* (The Lieutenant's Dog) and Sergi Belbel's *La Sang* (Blood), running in tandem at the experimental Sala Beckett, played to full houses for months.

Benet i Jornet's first play dates from 1963; by 1999, his published works numbered thirty-seven. He writes only in Catalan and has been widely translated, to Spanish and other languages. He has won several major prizes, including the Catalan Government's best play award for *Desig* (Desire), 1989, and the Spanish National Prize for Dramatic Literature for *E. R.*, 1995. Recently *E.R.* and *Testament* (*Legacy*) have been made into successful films directed by Ventura Pons and distributed in both Catalan and Spanish versions: "Actresses" (1997) and "Friend/ Lover" (1999).

The current flourishing of Catalan theatre began in 1985, coinciding with the premiere of Benet i Jornet's *La Desaparició de Wendy* (The Disappearance of Wendy), written some years earlier. The movement is characterized by an exploration of the theatricality of the text and is a departure from the independent, collective theatre of the 1960s and 1970s, which reflected a Brechtian influence in the use of art as a political instrument. The new approach is more skeptical and minimalist; in its use of mechanisms to purposely obscure the play, it follows in the tradition of Beckett and Pinter. Some of these techniques include breaching the linear structure of the story and essentializing characters. The characters' identity is defined by their dialogues and the contrasts established with the other

JOSEP M. BENET I JORNET
Photo by Pilar Aymerich

characters. They do not even have names. In *Legacy*, the main characters are the Young Man, the Friend, and the Professor.

In Benet i Jornet's earliest plays, the characters he constructed were more defined and realistic, in the traditional sense of the word. In this respect, *Desig* was an important turning point in his work. *Desig*, *Fugaç* (Fleeting), *E.R.*, *Testament*, *El Gos del Tinent* and *Precisament Avui* (Just Today), the works of the past decade, deal with contemporary concerns: the crisis of the couple, loneliness, terminal illnesses, the passing of time, the search for meaning and identity, violence, racism, and sexuality.

According to the playwright, *Legacy* is his most optimistic play. In it, he explores the possibility of passing one's moral and intellectual heritage to the next generation. To this end, he uses the image of the conceived child to synthesize opposite sides of society. He shows memory as the only way of preserving identity, since no written documents can be kept or trusted. Despite its optimism, especially manifest at the end, the play has a somber tone. Subtexts and occasional simultaneity of stories that the audience cannot really understand--phones which remain unanswered and apparently senseless dialogues--seem to shape a metaphor for general miscommunication and for the difficulty of fully comprehending life and personal relationships.

Eulàlia Borràs-Riba
EUETII-Universitat Politècnica de Catalunya

CAUTION: Professionals and amateurs are hereby warned that *Legacy*, being fully protected under the Copyright Laws of the United States of America, the British Empire, including the Dominion of Canada, and all other countries covered by the Pan-American Copyright Convention and the Universal Copyright Conventions, and of all countries with which the United States has reciprocal copyright relations, is subject to royalty. All rights, including professional, amateur, motion picture, recitation, public reading, radio and television broadcasting, and the rights of translation into foreign languages, are strictly reserved. Particular emphasis is laid on the question of readings, permission for which must be secured in writing.

Inquiries regarding permissions should be addressed to the author through

Alfredo Carrión Sáiz
Director de Artes Escénicas y Musicales
Sociedad General de Autores y Editores
Fernando VI, 4
28004 Madrid, SPAIN
Phone: 011-34-91-349 96 86   Fax: 011-34-91-349 97 12

or through the translator

Janet Ann DeCesaris
Universitat Pompeu Fabra
Departament de Traducció i Filologia
La Rambla, 30-32
08002 Barcelona, SPAIN
Phone: 011-34-93-542 22 48   Fax: 011-34-93-542 16 17
E-mail: janet.decesaris@trad.upf.es

Legacy at María Guerrero National Theatre in Madrid, 1996. Directed by Gerardo Vera. Photo by Ros Ribas.

Legacy received its world premiere at the María Guerrero National Theatre in Madrid on 14 March 1996, under the direction of Gerardo Vera. The Castilian translation, *Testamento*, was by Albert Ribas Pujol. The three actors were Juan Diego, Chete Lera, and Armando del Río.

The original Catalan version, *Testament*, premiered at the Romea Theatre in Barcelona on 28 June 1997, as part of the city's annual Festival Grec. It was directed by Sergi Belbel; the cast consisted of Lluís Soler, Jordi Boixaderas, and David Selvas.

CHARACTERS

YOUNG MAN
PROFESSOR
FRIEND

VOICES

PROLOGUE

The stage is dark. A blurring of indistinguishable sounds. Perhaps music, or words, or the hum of a city. As the sounds fade a phone conversation comes to the fore.

FEMALE VOICE: You are going to do it, aren't you? You have to get started.
MALE VOICE: I guess. Well, I'm going to at least begin. I have to do it. I want to, but. . .
FEMALE VOICE: What's the matter?
MALE VOICE: I don't know, it's not going to turn out right.
FEMALE VOICE: Oh, come on.
MALE VOICE: I'm not bright enough. If only. . . I'm not asking to be a great wit. Do you know what I'd really ask for, if I could? To know how to choose the precise word, the word that makes people listen. If I were convinced that I could ask with words, that I had the power to control words. . . If I. . . Just think, words that get to the heart, if only I could immerse myself in bright shining words. Well, no. I don't have that power, I'm not that kind of genius. How can I begin? Are you listening? How can I find the right way to. . . How am I going to get this going?

(The conversation fades and becomes confused with a new conversation, and then this new conversation dominates.)

VERY YOUNG MALE VOICE: Shut up, don't say such stupid things. I'm not going to listen.
MATURE MALE VOICE: Are you ashamed of me? You are what I love most in the world. The only thing I still hold on to.
VERY YOUNG MALE VOICE: Father, I don't want you to say that. Father, no.
MATURE MALE VOICE: Your life is my only commitment. You are my reflection.
VERY YOUNG MALE VOICE: I don't want to hear it! I'm gonna hang up. Did'ya hear me? I'm gonna hang up.
MATURE MALE VOICE: You're the only one who counts. And yet still I ask you to forgive me. Tomorrow. . . I can assure you that you won't understand the world any better than I. . . Son? Are you there?
VERY YOUNG MALE VOICE: Yeah, but you need to calm down. I want you to settle down. And don't make me feel ashamed. Don't make me feel ashamed, please.

(The conversation fades, and is replaced by another.)

1ST FEMALE VOICE: These are bad times.

2ND FEMALE VOICE: They're not very good, no, but that's the way it is. And do you know how you have to deal with them? If you don't screw them, they'll screw you. That's if you don't want to die.

1ST FEMALE VOICE: No way. I'm going to hold out if I can.

2ND FEMALE VOICE: Of course you're going to hold out. Just like me! Yours truly is not going die, nor am I going to let them get me! If what you have to do is go steal, well, I'll go steal. I'm going to do whatever I have to. No, I'm not going to let them get me, I tell you.

(The conversation fades, and becomes confused with and is then replaced by another that is, in fact, a monologue.)

OLD MALE VOICE: We used to sit down in a corner... anywhere. Somewhere we could see the sky... and we would chat. Yes, we chatted. We were young. What was beyond the city, the mountains, the sea, the sky? We were overcome by nostalgia. Nostalgia for what? For what, you ask? I have never understood where this nostalgia came from. (*Pause.*) We were young; we were kids, yet we were already nostalgic.

(The monologue fades, and is replaced by this last voice.)

MIDDLE-AGED FEMALE VOICE: You make me laugh. What are you waiting for? There is no hope, no future, no nothing. Sorry about that, but nothing. The truth is you always assume the opposite. But there's nothing. Sorry. Knowing this will help you keep on going with, oh, I don't know, a spark of serenity. Knowing this, that there's no future. None whatsoever.

SCENE ONE

Suddenly, three seconds of total silence, as the lights slowly come up. The distinct sound of a phone ringing. The recorded message of an answering machine responds.

ANSWERING MACHINE: Please leave your message at the sound of the beep.
INDECISIVE MALE VOICE: Uh. . . I'll call. . . I'll call later. It's just that, well, I saw. . .

(The voice goes silent abruptly, too abruptly. The lights are on and we are in the setting of the character we will call "YOUNG MAN". On the stage are the YOUNG MAN and the PROFESSOR, both standing still, as if they have just arrived.)

PROFESSOR: Your apartment. I'm glad I'm finally able to see it.
YOUNG MAN (*Unenthusiastically*): Yes.
PROFESSOR: While we were talking, you know I didn't even realize we took the elevator.
YOUNG MAN: I should have gone with you to your place, you know. To thank you and say good-bye at the door.
PROFESSOR: Well, the conversation was interesting and. . . these things happen.
YOUNG MAN: I know. But you are the professor and I am the student.
PROFESSOR: Oh. Biases. Perhaps I'm the one who should be biased.
YOUNG MAN: I've taken up too much of your time already. I don't mean just today. In the past few weeks. . .
PROFESSOR: The last few weeks. Precisely since you handed in your paper on the Catalan mystic Raymond Lully. I found it. . . How do you young people say it? Awesome.
YOUNG MAN (*Uncomfortable*): Awesome?
PROFESSOR: Awesome. An intelligent piece of work, you know. A personal view, without the usual textbook-like comments, and most curiously, without stupid statements. An intelligent paper about a writer who has little to do with us. Someone from the far-off medieval period, too far removed from what we might assume are your interests. In his time Raymond Lully was relevant to everyone, but today?. . . I read your damn paper and I felt. . . It seemed to me that. . . dammit, you're hardly an expert in thirteenth-century literature, and you know nothing about the rather odd philosophical system he was preaching about. A system that means nothing today. Just pure archaeology that is of interest to four highly educated, crazy people who live their field as if it were a sexual perversion. And here's where your glorious paper comes in, casting light on Lully's mysticism. You

made that prehistoric fossil come back to life, with blood running through the words he wrote so many centu-ries ago, full of faith and enthusiasm. I'm not talking about his verse. Your paper, as it were, saved Raymond Lully. You saved a dead man. You brought him back to life, however briefly. (*Pause.*) He spoke through you. He spoke as if he were alive--alive! And that's something that, frankly, I had not anticipated. He spoke through a young man like you, with a young man's sensitivity like yours. Well, that happens only once in a great while. An unassuming, inoffensive student arrives, opens his mouth and leaves you gaping.

YOUNG MAN: My paper on Raymond Lully was shit. Thank you for your interest. (*Change in tone.*) I have nothing to offer you. . . I live alone. You've wasted a lot of time with me today.

PROFESSOR: Yes, I must go. (*But he doesn't move, sure of himself, calm.*) I gave you a disk. (*Pause.*) The disk containing my essay. You said you had a computer.

YOUNG MAN: But why do you want me to read it? My opinion doesn't mean anything. My paper on Lully wasn't any good. You're the intellectual, not me. Give the disk to your colleagues. Why did you give it to *me*? Sorry.

PROFESSOR: I've already told you what I thought about your paper on Lully, but it was shit, if that's what you prefer. Now, I would like to have your opinion as a student with no standards, no knowledge about anything at all, of something I wrote. Think of it as a crazy request. Indulge an old man like me, will you?

YOUNG MAN: I don't understand your. . . your disk, your essay.

PROFESSOR (*Attentively*): You've started reading it?

YOUNG MAN (*A bit ashamed*): Yes.

PROFESSOR: You don't understand it.

YOUNG MAN (*Abruptly*): I'm not sure if I'm interested. I guess I don't understand it.

PROFESSOR: You're not interested.

YOUNG MAN: I don't. . . My opinion doesn't. . . (*Pause.*) You try to be. . . optimistic.

PROFESSOR: Do you think so?

YOUNG MAN: There's no solution.

PROFESSOR: When you honor me by finishing my. . . monograph, you'll be able to explain it to me better. (*Transition. Now, without enthusiasm.*) I'm leaving. (*He looks around the place intensely.*) You must have a fellowship.

YOUNG MAN: Yes.

PROFESSOR: You started your studies late. Do you work? To earn a living, I mean. The grant by itself isn't enough. You live by yourself in an apartment. How do you do it without a family to help you make ends meet?

YOUNG MAN: Who told you I don't have any family?

PROFESSOR: Your academic file.

YOUNG MAN: Are you familiar with the files of all your students?
PROFESSOR: No, just yours.
YOUNG MAN: Why? Because it's an unusual file? Out-of-the-ordinary?
PROFESSOR: Perhaps I haven't expressed myself clearly. You are an exceptional student.

(Pause.)

YOUNG MAN: My father... took a trip to Panama. He was carrying drugs. He was trying to, I mean. He got caught. He was put in prison. He was dying from the shame. But nobody dies from shame so he committed suicide. *(Laughing.)* Well, now my secret is out. You already knew that.
PROFESSOR: Did you get along with your father?
YOUNG MAN: He was poor. As poor as they come. He was trying to act smart. It wasn't the only mistake he made in his life. He believed in things. He... and he hanged himself. Good riddance. He believed in things. Ideas. Grand ideas. I don't have any grand ideas, none at all. Well, of course, I believe in, I like sex and I like to read. *(Defiantly.)* I'm not going to learn anything by reading. Reading teaches you nothing. Writers and literature professors think it does. Reading is a nice way to spend time. And nothing more. I like to read, you know. I've got to admit it, I like reading.
PROFESSOR: You read very well, and you know it.
YOUNG MAN: What do you want?
PROFESSOR: When you have finished reading my essay, I want you to tell me to what extent you think it's shit.
YOUNG MAN: I'm not going to think anything at all about it.
PROFESSOR: You still have not told me how you make a living. Your place is nice, nicer than that of most of your fellow students.
YOUNG MAN *(Tense)*: Why did you come to my place? Just because? Just because we were talking? Why did you come up here?
PROFESSOR *(Trapped)*: Are you sorry I came?
YOUNG MAN: I don't understand.
PROFESSOR *(Giving in)*: Well, I'd better go.
YOUNG MAN *(Quickly)*: I enjoy your class. I have a good time in your class. But when I finish my degree I'm not going to be a teacher, I'm not going to apply for university positions, I won't be a writer, I won't do anything that you or the others expect me to do.
PROFESSOR *(No transition)*: Your father was a good man.
YOUNG MAN: Yeah, right.
PROFESSOR *(Cautiously)*: Are you certain I can't help you?
YOUNG MAN: I always do whatever I want. Until it's over. No one can help me.

PROFESSOR: I'll try to keep that in mind. Perhaps I've learned my lesson. *(Suddenly, the phone rings. The YOUNG MAN is tense. One, two, three rings. The PROFESSOR has not moved.)* Aren't you going to pick it up?
YOUNG MAN: The answering machine is on. If it's important enough, they'll leave a message. And.... sometimes it's a wrong number.
PROFESSOR *(Ironically)*: Yes, one percent of the time.

(The answering machine has clicked on.)

YOUNG MAN'S VOICE: Please leave your message at the sound of the beep.
INDECISIVE MALE VOICE: Uh... I'll call... I'll call back later. It's that, well, I saw...

(The YOUNG MAN jumps to the telephone and abruptly turns the volume down all the way. The PROFESSOR, perplexed, looks at him guiltily, but remains defiant.)

PROFESSOR: I'm sorry. I would be pissed, too, if someone I didn't know charged into my private space without my having given him permission to do so. Good-bye.
YOUNG MAN *(Holding back a certain anger)*: Wait.
PROFESSOR: What is it?

(Pause.)

YOUNG MAN: I'll return your disk to you.
PROFESSOR *(Ironically)*: Ah, so I see, you don't need to finish reading it.
YOUNG MAN *(Matter-of-factly)*: I read the whole thing. I'll go and get it.

(The PROFESSOR cannot help but show surprise.)

PROFESSOR: You read it all?

(The YOUNG MAN exits. Pause. The phone rings again. Once, twice, three times. The answering machine clicks on but no voice is heard. The PROFESSOR goes to the phone and turns up the volume.)

YOUNG MAN'S VOICE:... message at the sound of the beep.
VOICE OF THE FRIEND *(The unemotional voice of an adult male)*: You're not there? As you know my daughter's pregnant. And, as you also know, she has those beliefs of hers. I must talk to you. No excuses and no way out. *(The YOUNG MAN enters in a hurry. He is holding a computer disk in his hand.)* I'll call back.

(The party at other end of the line hangs up. The PROFESSOR is doubly confused.)

PROFESSOR: I know that voice. I know it quite well.
YOUNG MAN *(Bursting out in anger)*: Get out! Get the fuck out of here! Yeah, I am pissed that someone I hardly know charges into my space!

(Pause.)

PROFESSOR *(In amazement)*: A child.
YOUNG MAN *(Furiously)*: I said get out of here!
PROFESSOR: Are you returning the disk? "The Lover loved the Beloved enough to believe everything he said. And the Lover longed to understand him so much that. . ." And here comes a passage I don't remember. And then it goes, more or less, " The Friend's love lay between belief and intelligence."
YOUNG MAN *(Aggressively)*: What the hell does your great mystic Lully have to do with this?
PROFESSOR: Believing irrationally or believing intelligently. I don't know which I prefer. Do you? *(Pause.)* I have no children. May I have the disk? What do you think?

(The YOUNG MAN breaks the disk, glaring into the PROFESSOR's eyes.)

YOUNG MAN *(Cynically)*: Oh, it broke. Fortunately your splendid essay is saved on the hard drive.
PROFESSOR *(Wearily)*: I can see what you thought of my essay.

(The PROFESSOR turns and exits. When he is off-stage, the YOUNG MAN cries out angrily.)

YOUNG MAN: I'm not going to have any children, either!

(The YOUNG MAN keeps on looking towards where the Professor was. He is tense, ready to pounce. The phone rings again. This time he doesn't wait for the answering machine. He grabs the phone.)

YOUNG MAN: Hello!
INDECISIVE MALE VOICE: Uh, hello. . . Excuse me. . . I called you a few minutes ago.

YOUNG MAN: (*Controlling himself, cordial in a quiet sort of way*): I wasn't home. . . And sometimes the answering machine plays funny games. Have you had any problems?
INDECISIVE MALE VOICE: No. . . Hey. . . We don't know each other. I saw . . . I saw. . .
YOUNG MAN (*Making the conversation easier*): Okay, okay. Consider we've been introduced. Is it for today?
INDECISIVE MALE VOICE: Tomorrow, if you can make it.
YOUNG MAN: Sure. We'll agree on the price. You can be sure of that.

(*Another phone conversation drowns out their voices. The YOUNG MAN continues talking while the new conversation goes on, without our hearing what he says for at least a moment, and then the lights go down. This anonymous phone conversation takes place with the stage blacked-out.*)

MALE VOICE: This might seem stupid, but. . . How are we going to understand each other if you're hiding things that worry you from me?
FEMALE VOICE (*Laughing nervously*): Uh-uh, it just looks that way to you, but I'm not. Really.
MALE VOICE: Are you sure? A worry isn't a fear, but it's almost a fear.
FEMALE VOICE: Absurd. Your imagination.
MALE VOICE: Let yourself go. (*Long pause.*) Look, once when I was little, I was asleep and I woke up and heard noises. It was dark. Little, fleeting noises. Somebody was moving, somebody was watching me and was going to fall on top of me sooner or later.
FEMALE VOICE: What makes you tell me this now?
MALE VOICE: I was so afraid. . . I was so afraid that, why not get it over with? I got up, I walked in the dark, ran into a door. . . I opened it and I gave myself over to evil.
FEMALE VOICE: (*Laughing nervously*) To evil?
MALE VOICE: Yes. And then. . . Then I saw something wonderful, the most wonderful thing in my life. (*Pause.*) I had let myself go. . . Let yourself go. Come on, let yourself go.

SCENE TWO

The lights come up towards the end of the previous phone conversation and in front of us is the setting of the character we will call "FRIEND." There is a newspaper on an end table. The FRIEND is talking on the telephone.

FRIEND: I know, I know. Stay with her as long as you have to. Does she want to talk? Do you think she'd talk to me?
WIFE'S VOICE: She's upset. It'll be better if she doesn't.
FRIEND: Tell her that it doesn't matter to us. She's awfully young.
WIFE'S VOICE: I will not tell her that. She thinks it's transcendental or something. We would only make matters worse.
FRIEND: The problem is that guy. Can she hear you?
WIFE'S VOICE: No.
FRIEND: I don't like him. He scares me, and I don't know why. I'll go talk to him.
WIFE'S VOICE: Are you sure?
FRIEND: Yes, just a brief chat. He shouldn't influence her decision, you know? Neither the situation nor whatever decision she makes is the issue; what bothers me is him. (*The apartment doorbell rings.*) There's someone at the door. It's probably our guest.
WIFE'S VOICE: Tell him I'm sorry I can't be there. Make up some excuse.
FRIEND: Okay. Take care of her. Tell her I love her. (*He hangs up. He goes and opens the door, and returns with the PROFESSOR.*) Welcome to our home. Come on in. There's just the two of us.
PROFESSOR (*Not displaying the irritating self-assurance he exhibited in the Young Man's presence*): Your wife's not home?
FRIEND: No. She's very sorry. A last-minute problem. An... an elderly relative of hers, an aunt, took ill and she had to go and take care of her.
PROFESSOR: I'm sorry. Why didn't you tell me? We can get together at another time.
FRIEND: No, it's okay.
PROFESSOR: No, really. Let's leave it for another time. I'll come back.
FRIEND: No, please stay. We can have a long talk, like we used to.
PROFESSOR: Are you sure? I don't want to be a bother.
FRIEND: Would you be quiet and sit down and get comfortable, please? We're better off alone, anyway. At least this once. We won't have to worry about boring my wife to tears. Besides, we can celebrate that you're staying in the country.
PROFESSOR: That doesn't warrant a celebration.
FRIEND: You made us sweat it out. You've been playing around with the university for how long now? Three months?
PROFESSOR: I wasn't playing around. I couldn't make up my mind.

FRIEND: You signed the contract and we've got you now for a long time. Now it's your turn to tremble. I'm very pleased. You can think whatever you want, but I'm very pleased.

PROFESSOR: I don't have any more doubts. It was the students. Surprisingly, what convinced me was the students.

FRIEND: No kidding?

PROFESSOR: As usual most are pretty ignorant, like everywhere else. But, curiously, I felt comfortable with them. Especially with the class for majors, the medieval literature seminar. I won't be so lucky next year, if I'm still alive, but on the whole they're hard workers.

FRIEND (*Suddenly uncomfortable*): Yeah, sure.

PROFESSOR: Yes, really hard workers. (*Pause. He looks at the FRIEND a little maliciously.*) Some of them, you know, there's one... There's one exceptional one.

FRIEND: Not that exceptional.

PROFESSOR: You don't know them.

FRIEND (*Tersely*): Yes I do. I know them all too well. All of them.

PROFESSOR (*Openly provocative*): Then you must know who I'm talking about. A young man with great possibilities. A bright future if he wanted and if he weren't so unsociable, even unpleasant on occasion. His family background explains that, I guess.

FRIEND: He's an idiot.

PROFESSOR: You know who I mean?

FRIEND: A well of arrogance. Oh, his woeful past! We'll make every allowance for him, won't we, with a family background as sorrowful as his?

PROFESSOR: You do know who I mean.

FRIEND: I agree he's smart. And bad company, incapable of getting along with others, incapable of bringing himself close to others.

PROFESSOR (*Starting to enjoy himself*): The best student. No, it doesn't have anything to do with his being a student. He is the person who is most capable of understanding everything that I've met in years.

FRIEND (*Emphatically*): I can't stand him. (*More calmly.*) Let's not waste time talking about him, okay? This is supposed to be a quiet get-together of two friends who want to remember when they were younger and when, well, you know.

PROFESSOR: All right. Let's change topics. (*Pretending to make chit-chat.*) And your daughter? When did she move out?

FRIEND (*Irritated*): My daughter?

PROFESSOR: Yes.

FRIEND (*Recovering*): She moved to a ridiculously tiny apartment to hang out with an indefinite number of enthusiastic friends of both sexes. Here she didn't have

enough space, since there were only three of us. The day after she turned eighteen, good-bye. You're lucky to not have children.
PROFESSOR (*Now it's his turn to be irritated, even though the Friend spoke without an ulterior motive*): Don't say stupid things! (*Pensively.*) A child.
FRIEND (*Changing topics*): Well, no matter what, I'm glad you're happy at the university, after you taught all over, everywhere, for so many years. Those countless clowns didn't deserve someone like you.
PROFESSOR: The final refuge.
FRIEND: Listen, I'm sorry but I haven't had a chance to read your essay yet. I'm dying to read it, but I just haven't been able to. The disk is next to the computer and I promise I'll get to it tomorrow.
PROFESSOR: You're not going to like it.
FRIEND: Of course not. Don't be modest.
PROFESSOR: It's, well, it's like that student in the seminar, only in reverse.
FRIEND: You're comparing your essay to a clod? What would you like to drink?
PROFESSOR: Vodka.
FRIEND: You're drinking vodka? Since when? I don't have any vodka.
PROFESSOR: Then mineral water.
FRIEND: Are you trying to make things difficult for me?
PROFESSOR: Gin.
FRIEND: Now you've got it. I have gin. We have to get drunk as we recall all the memories and mistakes of our youth.
PROFESSOR: We will recall an old, faded fondness.
FRIEND: We will recall fondness that has not faded away.
PROFESSOR: Fondness, love, affection. Someone who needs you. It's all over when nobody needs you. Do you still need me?
FRIEND: You're asking a lot. Yes. And why not? Yes, most definitely. Here's to your health. A toast to the honorable professor who has come home after I don't know how many years of exile.
PROFESSOR: To your health. For my health it's a bit too late. All these years I worked a reasonable amount, I fucked a reasonable amount. . . but I was never committed to anyone. Or, at least I never believed I was committed to anyone. Well, I fell in love a couple of times. It didn't last, you know. And I was homesick. That's why I came back, albeit too late.
FRIEND: What do you mean too late?
PROFESSOR: I'm ill. Or so it seems.
FRIEND: You're a hypochondriac.
PROFESSOR: Right. I was able to finish the essay. To come back, to get it published and then the rest doesn't matter.
FRIEND: What do you mean you're ill?

PROFESSOR (*Ironically*): I might not die. (*Imitating a doctor talking to him.*) "Just think, today we have very sophisticated medical treatments available. The possibilities of failure are very small, very remote. Don't worry unnecessarily." If they had only said, "Look, you have six months, a year, two years, three years left." Or even, "Go to hell and don't come back, you're finished." But they decided they didn't want to scare the patient. In other words, I am absolutely terrified at night and I have to keep quiet when someone refers to me as a hypochondriac because, of course, he might be right.

(*Pause.*)

FRIEND (*Devastated*): I'm sorry. God, I'm very sorry.
PROFESSOR: Thanks for your tone of voice. I might even think you meant it.
FRIEND: You idiot! I would feel awful if something happened to you. Don't you know that or what? Are you my friend or not? Too many years of putting up with each other, even if it was by mail most of the time. Like a marriage by correspondence. The day one of us is gone, the other is going to be screwed. I know that, and so do you. So try not to act like a fool, okay? Take the medicine and listen to the doctors. Don't let the fact that they're a bunch of illiterates get to you. Behave yourself or else I'm going to get mad.
PROFESSOR: Just in case, the essay is finished. You're not going to like it, but be patient.
FRIEND: You're a liar, but I'll be patient.
PROFESSOR: It doesn't bother me so much now if you don't like what I wrote. It was different when we were students. You were my teacher. You, not the professors, were my real teacher. You told me what books I should read--some of which were unbearable--and you taught me. I could never understand, I still can't understand why you were so patient with me.
FRIEND: There was something about you. Some charm, a certain clarity of thought, and you knew how to listen. I don't know.
PROFESSOR: I was a real jerk in those days. I can't stand people who are jerks. It would only have made sense if you had loved me.
FRIEND: I did love you.
PROFESSOR: Let's be specific. I was the one who loved you.
FRIEND: Don't start on that.
PROFESSOR: To be more precise, I was the one who lusted for you.

(*Pause.*)

FRIEND (*Uncomfortable*): Some things are best left unsaid.

PROFESSOR: We're big boys now. You've always known, even if nothing was ever put into words.
FRIEND: So now what do you want?
PROFESSOR: To talk. Wasn't this supposed to be a session devoted to old times? I just want to talk. Doctors. Who can believe doctors? I want to come clean. I have been to bed with many. . . No, with a considerable. . . With a certain number of men, and you have enjoyed yourself immensely every time I told you about my idiotic adventures. Love, what you might call love, just a couple of guys. And right now. . . (*Pause.*) But there was always something in the air that couldn't be said. The fact is you are the one I have wanted and loved most in my life.
FRIEND (*Taking it with a smile*): I don't deserve the honor.
PROFESSOR: Well, before today I never would have told you. I was happy for you with your girlfriends, and I was even happier when you got married, because you married the right woman. Your wife is fantastic. Your mutual fidelity over time is one of the most curious, incomprehensible, tender and marvelous relationships I have ever witnessed. For long periods of time at night, in bed, I have lived with my loneliness, my desperation.
FRIEND (*Softly*): Oh, get off it.
PROFESSOR: Just like a good romance novel. No, just like everyone always ends up saying one day of someone, you were the great love of my life. And you knew it. But I didn't spoil things. If I had let myself tell you, we would not have continued being friends, comrades-in-arms who have a grand ol' time judging the world from their mutual complicity, etcetera, etcetera. Sometimes I think that with the tenderness you felt for me it wouldn't have been difficult for us one day to have ended up in bed. But if that had happened, afterwards our friendship would have been shot to hell. And I didn't want that, I had decided to keep our friendship at all cost, for ever and ever. It was awful for me, but I did it.
FRIEND: Awful? Aren't you exaggerating a bit? I refuse to admit that I behaved like a thoughtless, self-centered person.
PROFESSOR: I loved you so much, you fool. But calm down, everything comes to an end. There are dregs at the bottom, and that's all there is. In fact, my romantic life has been, overall, more active than yours, so please spare me the anxiety attack. Especially if the result has to be total inertia when faced with the prospect of. . . I hope you will invite me here to your home from now on whenever necessary, with the proper regularity for two kindred souls. No kidding.
FRIEND: Just a minute. I want, I want to get things straight with you. Since you have started.
PROFESSOR: You want to get things straight? Oh God, now what are you going to say? How are you going to punish me for having broken the taboo?
FRIEND: Will you shut up, damn it! I don't even know what affection is.
PROFESSOR: Shared self-centeredness.

FRIEND: That's one possible definition. Well then, affection means nothing, but I've only spread it around seven or eight people over all these years. And one of them is you. I have never wanted to get involved with you. I am a conventional male. Of course, you might be right. In any event, are you sure it would make any difference?
PROFESSOR: It depends. (*Pause.*) No. (*Pause.*) Thanks. (*Transition.*) Sure. The book, my intellectual exercise, is not going to be to your liking. It took me six months to write it. In record time. This intellectual exercise of mine. I didn't print it out. It's only on disk. I'm looking forward to your corrections.
FRIEND: You began writing it. . . When you began did you know about your illness?
PROFESSOR (*Attentively*): Yes.
FRIEND: From what you've said about the essay, what I'm not going to like is being confronted by a book written out of fear.
PROFESSOR: Aha.
FRIEND: Life runs from here to here. No longer. And that's enough. I'm glad I lived. You're also glad you lived. We agree on that, don't we? Those pathetic people who have spent their lives saying that dead dogs don't bite, and then suddenly, whether right or wrong, they see the end coming and start to claim some sort of transcendence because they're scared shitless, well, they think they're too important to accept that they can just disappear. I won't like it if you. . . (*HE shuts up.*)
PROFESSOR: The essay doesn't discuss transcendence. At least not like you think it does. It talks about a legacy. The story of a man. A piece of matter who knows himself, who can be shocked and who can be hurt. And who disappears. His legacy is pain. I wonder if the end of each individual person is the same as that of humanity in general. Yes, absolutely. But no, nothing is sure. Not even that. Maybe an heir will save us some day from pain. An heir who will spring up from us but who won't be like us. Someone as incomprehensible for me as I am for a dog.
FRIEND: Even more so. At least the dog can see you, but you can't see this science-fiction heir of yours. There is no heir.
PROFESSOR: You're probably right. But I can't help it. I'm interested in those who come after me, even if I can't understand them. For example, I'm interested in the young man who got your daughter pregnant.

(*Pause.*)

FRIEND: Wow, that was a nice counterpunch. More like a low blow. How did you find out?
PROFESSOR: I was at his place when you called. I recognized your voice immediately.

FRIEND: My wife is with my daughter. My daughter doesn't know how to make decisions. She's not even nineteen yet! She can go to bed with whomever she wants, but I can't stand your brilliant student! I can't stand him! And what's strange is that she is, well, confused. She doesn't know what to do. I think she wants his opinion.
PROFESSOR: I'm scared of dying, so I write some pitiful lines. What are you so scared of?
FRIEND: Not of anything absurd, esoteric, or incomprehensible. I'm just your average father. I'm afraid that my daughter, an indiscriminate teenager, is creating problems for herself by having a child who, to top things off, is the offspring of a mean, irresponsible, disagreeable, antisocial bastard! A bastard. I've had him in class, too, but his physical attributes didn't get to me.
PROFESSOR: But they did to me.
FRIEND: That would appear to be the case.
PROFESSOR: I'm tired. We've had enough fun. I'm leaving.
FRIEND: No!
PROFESSOR: We get along better in writing.
FRIEND: Don't go! Can't I even fight with you for a while? If you're tired I can give you some, well, what do you have to take?
PROFESSOR: I'm not leaving because I'm mad. You've got more reason to be upset than I do. But enough is enough for today. The fact is I'm not tired. Not at all. Not tired, not angry. But I am horny, and that's the truth. You might think I'm impertinent, but the conversation, the memories, and the arguments haven't angered me, they've aroused me.
FRIEND: Oh, come on.
PROFESSOR: Very much so, to be precise. The body's reactions are unpredictable.
FRIEND: I really don't know how to take you.
PROFESSOR: Just let me leave. I'll find a way to have some real fun. Will you get around to reading the essay once your daughter has made up her mind?
FRIEND: I'll get to it right away, regardless of my daughter. But don't leave yet. Stop being so difficult, will you?
PROFESSOR: All right. Get me some aspirin. Better yet, get me a cup of coffee.
FRIEND: Done.

(The FRIEND exits. The PROFESSOR picks up a newspaper on top of the end table and starts turning the pages at random. Suddenly HE stops and stares at something. HE smiles. HE goes over to the telephone with the newspaper in his hand and dials a number. Someone answers.)

VOICE: Hello.

PROFESSOR: I was looking through the personal ads in the newspaper. Your ad is intriguing. "Choose between fucking and making love." That's why I decided to call you. Can you come over in half an hour? If I don't like you I'll pay your cab fare home and bye-bye. If I like you, we fuck. I don't care how much you charge. I do care that you give everything as promised. My address is... *(The FRIEND walks in just at this moment with the cup of coffee.)* Sorry. I'll call back in a minute. *(The PROFESSOR hangs up.)*
FRIEND: Who were you calling?
PROFESSOR: Nobody.
FRIEND: Nobody. My kind of guy. Here's your coffee. *(The telephone rings. The FRIEND picks it up.)* Hello.
WIFE'S VOICE: It's me. I suppose you're not alone.
FRIEND: That's right. How's it going?
WIFE'S VOICE: No change.
FRIEND: Oh.
WIFE'S VOICE: I'd be having more fun with you two.
FRIEND *(To the PROFESSOR)*: It's my wife. Do you want to talk to her?
PROFESSOR: No. I left some time ago. Tell her I'm sorry her aunt took ill.
FRIEND: What aunt?
PROFESSOR: The one you told me was sick.
FRIEND: Son of a bitch! Stick around. The coffee.
PROFESSOR: You drink it before it gets cold. We got carried away, and it's all my fault. That's enough for today. I need some fresh air.
WIFE'S VOICE: What's going on?
FRIEND *(Into the telephone):* Wait. *(To the PROFESSOR.)* I'll give you a call tomorrow. Very sick, but you're going out on the town, aren't you? You're all I needed at this point! *(The PROFESSOR smiles at him, waves good-bye, and exits. The FRIEND goes back to talking on the telephone.)* He just left.
WIFE'S VOICE: Wasn't he just there with you?
FRIEND: He was here, but he just left. What about her?
WIFE'S VOICE: Waiting for some sort of inspiration.
FRIEND: Waiting for that stupid stud, that irresponsible prick who couldn't even take the necessary steps to prevent... Oh God, just listen to me talk. Why did you call?
WIFE'S VOICE: I needed to.
FRIEND: You needed me. I need you. We need each other. You and me. At least you and me. Friendship is something else. Friendship is... another story.

(The sound of another phone conversation drowns out his voice. As the new phone conversation takes place, the FRIEND continues talking with his wife for at least a moment, without our hearing what they say, and then blackout. The

conversation between a MALE VOICE and a FEMALE VOICE takes place with the lights down.)

YOUNG FEMALE VOICE: We're lucky we can say we're still friends, you know? We still have that.

MALE VOICE: That's not enough. I love you. You've slammed the door and made love disappear. Your slam and a gust of frigid air.

YOUNG FEMALE VOICE: Don't make me pity you. You like to exaggerate. Words.

MALE VOICE: Yeah, say whatever you want. A gust of frigid air. And to get warm again, you know what? I have tried grasping onto the memory of moments with people I love, not just of you. I've found a few. But I know you weren't able to live those moments of fulfillment. No, not then. I have only been able to find fulfillment and comfort on the odd winter afternoon, when the sun comes through the window and touches my shoulder blade. Love. You've left me. And now where will I find love?

Legacy, in Madrid, 1996. Photo by Ros Ribas.

SCENE THREE

Towards the end of the previous phone conversation the lights come up and we are in the PROFESSOR'S setting. There is a computer. The PROFESSOR has changed clothes; some minor change, perhaps, that he thinks looks nice. He sits in front of the computer and turns it on. He uses the mouse to give commands until a text appears on the screen. He seems to be reading it. And he does not look satisfied; rather, he looks anxious. The doorbell rings. He turns the computer off. He unconsciously smooths his clothes, but reacts with skepticism. He opens the door. The YOUNG MAN appears. Dead silence. The YOUNG MAN is casually dressed. Even though it corresponds to a stereotype, his physical attractiveness is purposefully highlighted. They look at each other and take some time to react.

PROFESSOR: What are you doing here?
YOUNG MAN (*Cautiously, but with a slight tinge of hostility*): I don't think I have the wrong address.
PROFESSOR: I think you do. You must have made a mistake, no matter what.
YOUNG MAN: Yes, it was your voice. You called a number listed in the personal ads. Twice. You called a personal ad listed in the newspaper. (*With no feeling.*) You have requested the services of a male prostitute. I see customers either at my place or wherever they tell me. You wanted me to come here. No problem, it'll cost you a little more. But you don't care about the price. The hustler you called was me.
PROFESSOR: No, it must be a mistake.
YOUNG MAN: Are you ashamed to admit you pay for sex? Don't worry, I won't tell anyone. I'm beginning to understand you better now. But why should you, who's been around, feel ashamed of yourself?
PROFESSOR: Shame. At this point I don't know what that is. It's you. You're the problem. You're not gay.
YOUNG MAN (*Laughing a little*): I'm not?
PROFESSOR: You got a girl pregnant.
YOUNG MAN: I'm not prejudiced. My interest in sex knows no bounds. What about yours? Too bad, you know, you don't know what you're missing. Of course, I'm not interested in long-term relationships with anybody. No ties. Other people can be misled, but it's not my fault. I'm a loner and I go wherever the wind takes me.
PROFESSOR: When it comes to prostitution, you only do it with men. There was nothing ambiguous about the ad.
YOUNG MAN: Most of the people answering the ad are men. And I like men. Is the questioning over? I didn't know you were a queer, either. I should've guessed. Let's get on with it, okay? If I'm your type, that is. And remember that you pay up front. Well, I suppose I can trust you.

(The YOUNG MAN starts to undress.)

PROFESSOR: Wait a minute.
YOUNG MAN: Relax. You're not the professor now and I'm not the student. Now you're my customer, and the customer always gets his way. I can make suggestions, if you want, of course. Take your shirt off, first. *(Pause. The PROFESSOR does not move.)* You have to take it off. Do you want me to do it?

(The PROFESSOR slowly removes his shirt. The YOUNG MAN has already done so. Contrast between the young, fresh body of the YOUNG MAN and the older, worn body of the PROFESSOR.)

PROFESSOR *(Slowly)*: That's why you have your own apartment. A nicer place than most students have that don't live at home. Despite your father's being just a poor guy who thought that there was meaning to the world, and when he stopped believing in that he botched things up and hanged himself.
YOUNG MAN: Keep on going. As long as you pay, you can do whatever you want. You want to hurt me? Okay, go right ahead. I'm a professional. You won't be sorry. What am I going to be thinking about to get me hot while I look at and hug your skin, your flesh that the years have taken their toll on? The hookers can fake it easier. You ought to work out. It's not too late for you. Don't worry, I'll get it up. You can even think I find you attractive. I'm a true pro. You're gonna have a great time. Keep on going, don't stop. You were talking about my father.
PROFESSOR *(Who has stopped undressing)*: Why do you do it?
YOUNG MAN *(About to unbutton his pants, but he stops)*: What?
PROFESSOR: You don't need to. You could get by doing something else. I don't understand you at all.
YOUNG MAN: What are you talking about? What's with you? You don't have to understand me. Use me. If you're not ashamed, then what is it? Do you have something against me? A man who turns his students on by uncovering the perversity in literature, and now you're shocked?
PROFESSOR: Listen to me. I loved the same person for a very long time. Too long. I got over it. I fell in love two more times, but neither lasted as long as the first. And now, the class, the seminar at the university. It was temporary. I wasn't sure I was going to stay on. One day, you, of all your classmates, stood up, hostile, unbearable, and you started to talk. What you said... You were looking through the dust in the air. The particles you could see in the light from the window. You were talking. What you were saying had nothing to do with what I thought, nor with what I felt. Surprisingly enough, what you said made sense. I can never catch you, but that's what it's all about, and what you said had a sort of odd logic to it. As I was listening to your comments on a text by I don't know whom--I don't think

it was Lully--as I was listening to the astonishing atrocities of your claims, I discovered, amidst the dust and the words, your face and body. I was sure it was never going to happen to me again. I signed the contract. You are why I am going to stay at the university. I'm in love with you.

(Pause.)

YOUNG MAN: Poor guy. It's over. You're through. You'll never be loved by anyone. Never again. Never. Nobody's going to feel for you or love you. Never again. You're going to have to pay for sex. And if you're lucky you might find a professional like me, who'll make you enjoy yourself, who'll make you feel good every time you call. But no feelings. No one to tremble when you get close, no one to say "I love you" as a bitter sensation slides down from your neck and your dick hardens in shame. No more of that.

(Pause.)

PROFESSOR: Thank you for the information.

(The PROFESSOR slowly puts his shirt back on. He is tired but not defeated.)

YOUNG MAN *(Feigning innocence)*: Shit, I took the wind out of your sail. I just lost a customer.
PROFESSOR: You did not.
YOUNG MAN: I broke the ground rules of the turf. Too bad for me, now I won't get paid. *(He puts his shirt back on.)* I'm sorry, professor. Really. If you want I can get you another guy you'll take to, first-class material. I know some guys who are more worth the trouble than me. *(In a neutral tone.)* I apologize. You don't have to accept my apology. Because I'm leaving.
PROFESSOR: No.
YOUNG MAN: What?
PROFESSOR: Please don't go.
YOUNG MAN: You've got to be kidding. Are you still suggesting. . . ?
PROFESSOR: Nothing about sex. I'm in love with you and you've already told me what I can expect. No sex. So, I'm weak now. Why not? Perhaps I will, I really will let you introduce me to some guy who does the same thing you do. Someone who used to. . . Don't worry, I'm not angry.
YOUNG MAN: What do you want, then?
PROFESSOR: To make a deal. I want. . . that is to say. . . I suppose the expression is to help you. Yes, I want to help you.
YOUNG MAN: Help me.

PROFESSOR: Listen and let me explain. A business contract. You get out of prostitution. I have nothing against prostitution, I use it myself, but it's not for you. Let's see, how can we formalize my help? A sort of scholarship, you might say. You keep on studying and it makes no difference if you do not want to become a writer or teacher or whatever else naïve students in the humanities want to be. Time will tell. There is one condition, however. (*Pause.*) Try to convince the girl you got pregnant to have the child.

(*Pause.*)

YOUNG MAN (*Indignant upon hearing the last sentence*): I could throw up all over you and you'd still thank me? The child! I am not going to have a child! You didn't understand anything, did you? You're not going to buy me, you fag. I know what I'm going to do with my own life. I'm not blind, you know. I know where I am. This is my plan. I'm going to read, I'm going to screw--for pleasure or for money-- and I'm going to fuck whatever I feel like, whoever I want. No ties to anyone. And the day I look at myself in the mirror and I see myself half as worn as you, the day I start feeling ashamed of my body, on that day, I tell you, I'm going to kill myself. Yeah, just like my dear ol' dad, and so what? At least I won't have let myself be deceived, like he did, because I won't have believed in anything and I'll have had a damned good time doing it! You get it, or do you want me to rewind the tape?

PROFESSOR: You're not going to do that. You can talk about suicide since it's a long way off. It sounds good. But no. You talk too much. Why the hell do you, of all people, have to commit suicide? You'll cling to life dearly. You're smart, you know how to read, you're sexy and I'm smitten with you. But careful now, I'm not blind either. You're no star-crossed romantic hero. No, you're not. You'll cling to life dearly. One day you'll get a pot belly and then in a hurry you'll search for all sorts of wonderful justifications to go on living. Who are you kidding? Your father, that unhappy man, believed in things, and yes, that is precisely why he was able to kill himself!

YOUNG MAN: You don't know a thing about my father!

PROFESSOR: Be quiet! He believed, and that's why he committed suicide! You don't have his excuse. Look at me! Me, the college professor; you, selling men's underwear in some store! That's what differentiates your future from mine! Otherwise, we're just the same. You won't have the balls to kill yourself!

YOUNG MAN: Shut up!

PROFESSOR: Act smart, and make a deal with me!

YOUNG MAN: Shove it up your ass, that's what you like, anyway!

PROFESSOR: A future selling "undergarments for the discriminating man." You have taste, you'll do just fine.

YOUNG MAN: You son of a bitch!

(The YOUNG MAN jumps the PROFESSOR, hitting and punching him. The PROFESSOR does not know how to, or does not want to, or cannot, defend himself.)

PROFESSOR (*Amidst the punches*): A deal! No! Stop, stop, you idiot! A deal!
YOUNG MAN: You want me to tear you apart? Will you shut up? Will you shut up?

(Finally, the YOUNG MAN lets the Professor go. The PROFESSOR falls to the ground, bleeding, his clothes ripped, looking a mess. The YOUNG MAN, extremely tense, turns his back to him, and lets out an almost animal-like sob.)

PROFESSOR (*Not breathing well, gasping*): So much violence, I might end up thinking, I might think that you feel something for me. It would never have occurred to me. (*Pause.*) A deal. You will have a child. I don't understand you. It doesn't matter. It will have to be this way. From now to. . . hundreds of thousands of years from now. . . who knows, maybe one chance in a billion. . . Maybe the children of your children's children will save you and me from pain. It's then that my shitty, cowardly monograph will have meaning. A meaning I can't even dream of. Raymond Lully could not, could never have imagined the meaning his words had coming from your mouth.
YOUNG MAN (*Angrily*): Your essay?
PROFESSOR (*As he tries to dry his wounds*): And you're not even aware of it. Yes, you do like me.
YOUNG MAN: So I like you, huh? And I'm going to make a deal with you, right? (*He turns to the computer.*) Is this where you store your precious essay, on the computer's hard drive?
PROFESSOR: That's where I save my work, yes.

(Without thinking twice, the YOUNG MAN grabs some substantial object and starts pounding the computer--or maybe he'll just kick it--and completely destroys it. The PROFESSOR looks on without getting up from the floor.)

PROFESSOR: Idiot, what are you doing? It's no use!

(But the YOUNG MAN has already destroyed the computer.)

YOUNG MAN (*Sarcastically, shaking*): A deal! There is no more essay and I committed a crime! A deal! You lost, there's not going to be any deal! I imagine I'll be hearing from you. From the police, too, I bet?

(The YOUNG MAN exits in a huff. Pause. The PROFESSOR, shivering, impatient, drags himself to the telephone. HE dials a number.)

FRIEND'S VOICE: Hello. Who's calling?
PROFESSOR: I need. . . I need to see you again.
FRIEND'S VOICE: Who is this?
PROFESSOR: It's. . .
FRIEND'S VOICE: What's wrong? You sound. . .
PROFESSOR: This isn't the time, but I need to go back to your place now.
FRIEND'S VOICE: What's the matter? Do you want me to come get you?
PROFESSOR: No, I'll come over there. I have to see you. I need. . . I need. .

(The sound of another phone conversation drowns out their voices. As the new phone conversation takes place, the PROFESSOR continues talking with the Friend for at least a moment, without our hearing what they say, and then blackout. The conversation between a MALE VOICE and a FEMALE VOICE takes place with the lights down.)

YOUNG MALE VOICE: Is that you? Hey, is it you?
YOUNG FEMALE VOICE: Can you hear me? I need. . . I need for you to understand me!
YOUNG MALE VOICE: Can you hear me? I can't hear very well!. There's some interference.
YOUNG FEMALE VOICE: We gotta talk.
YOUNG MALE VOICE: I feel bad about it. Yeah, please, we gotta talk! Speak up, and more slowly!
YOUNG FEMALE VOICE: I can't shout any louder! Can you hear me?
YOUNG MALE VOICE: Your voice keeps coming and going. It comes and then goes again.
YOUNG FEMALE VOICE: I can't do anything about it. There's nothing more to do. You can't hear me, there's no way to make you hear me! You only have two ears and they don't reach anywhere!
YOUNG MALE VOICE: Don't go so fast! What did you say?
YOUNG FEMALE VOICE: You only have two eyes and two ears to understand me with. Even if you were here, next to me, you still wouldn't understand me.!
YOUNG MALE VOICE: I don't get you, I don't get you at all. Wait!
YOUNG FEMALE VOICE: You won't understand me, so forget it, you won't understand me. What can we understand if we only have two eyes and two ears?

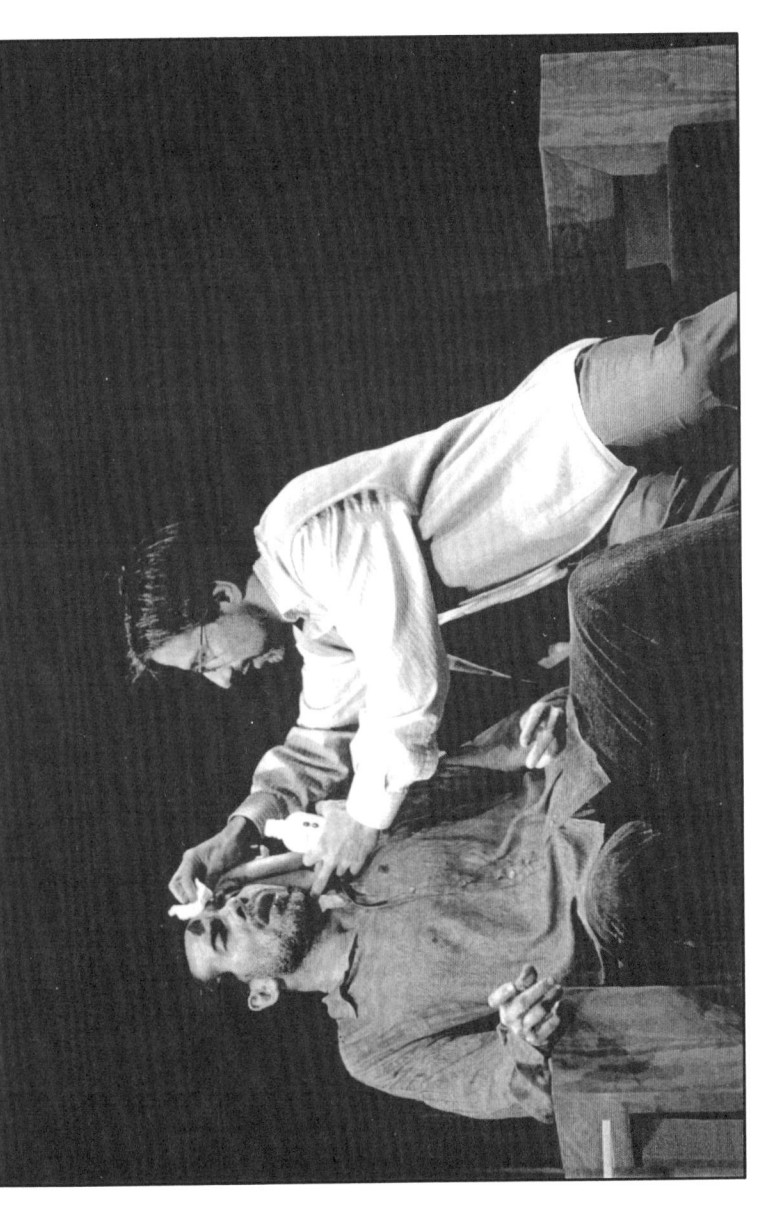

Legacy at Romea Theatre in Barcelona, 1997. Directed by Sergi Belbel. Photo by Pilar Aymerich.

SCENE FOUR

Towards the end of the telephone conversation the lights come up and we are now in the presence of the FRIEND's setting. The FRIEND comes on stage, practically holding up the PROFESSOR, who is still beat up and bleeding, as in the previous scene.

FRIEND: You have to go to the hospital. Right now. I'll go with you.
PROFESSOR: No, no. . .
FRIEND: You might have a broken bone. . . What do I know? Good God, you look like hell.
PROFESSOR: Let me sit down. I won't keep you long.
FRIEND: What do you mean you won't keep me long? Are you crazy? We're getting in the car and going straight to the emergency room.
PROFESSOR: I said no. Bring me a towel.
FRIEND: No. Are you quite certain I don't have to take you to the hospital?
PROFESSOR: Quite a mess but it doesn't matter. A towel please. . .

(The FRIEND exits and speaks for a moment from off-stage. Afterwards he enters on stage with a towel and some rubbing alcohol.)

FRIEND: You have to file charges. Who did this to you?
PROFESSOR: Don't make me nervous.
FRIEND: Why don't you want to go to the hospital? Because you don't want the police to find out? Are you involved in something illegal?
PROFESSOR: Yes.
FRIEND: You're crazy. *(HE is now next to the PROFESSOR.)* Let me take a look at it and clean it up as best as I can. Was it really that nonsense that occurred to you before you left? That you were horny and I don't know what else?
PROFESSOR: Yes.
FRIEND: You ended up with an asshole. Were you robbed? I'll bet he stole your wallet. What a screwed up life! Is it always like this? Pardon the question. I'm just a normal guy with no exciting experiences to impress friends with.
PROFESSOR: Calm down, nobody stole anything. You sound like my mother warning me to stay out of bad company. I don't feel all that bad, after all.
FRIEND: Do you want some gin, since there's no vodka?
PROFESSOR: Fine. But I'm only going to stay a minute. You have your own problems and you can rest after I've gone. I came, well, I came for two reasons. The first is I want you to give me the disk back.
FRIEND: What disk? You mean your disk? What do you need your disk for?

PROFESSOR: You have to give it back to me.
FRIEND: I haven't read it yet. I need to read it. I can't give it back yet.
PROFESSOR: You must return it to me. I need it.
FRIEND: Are you angry because of my biting comments about its probable contents? Are you punishing me or what?
PROFESSOR: Stop acting stupid.
FRIEND: You call up as if you're on fire, you get here half dead, you refuse to see a doctor or file a police report. . . And the only thing you're interested in is the goddam disk? How am I supposed to stop acting stupid?
PROFESSOR: The disk, please.
FRIEND: I have it here. There it is. Now what? You're going to just take it and run away, with no explanation at all, none whatsoever, no matter how asinine? Shit, even if you lie to me, you owe me some explanation.
PROFESSOR: Wait. I'm not leaving yet. I have to ask you for something else. Well, nothing else. I mean no other thing. But it affects you and I shouldn't get involved.
FRIEND: What is it?
PROFESSOR: If I've understood things properly, your daughter hasn't made up her mind to get an abortion.
FRIEND: What?
PROFESSOR: Does she want an abortion or not?
FRIEND: What are you driving at now? The decision will be made.
PROFESSOR: Having an abortion is the sensible solution and no further discussion is necessary. (*Pause.*) But I wish the child could be born.
FRIEND: What? Are you nuts?
PROFESSOR: At the root of this. . . There's you and there's that boy. I don't know what I'd give to see that child born. Your heir. And mine too, you know.
FRIEND: What are you saying?
PROFESSOR: I was in love with you for many, many years. And now I'm in love with that boy.
FRIEND: Just great! I thought so. Your mouth watered every time he was mentioned. He's a no good bastard.
PROFESSOR: I am afraid of death, you know that. And in this new life, you and he are intertwined. . .
FRIEND: No, no blackmail. And much less for something this twisted and stupid-assed. My heir and yours! Those are words! Words! But this asshole must have filled my daughter's head, not to mention her belly, with smoke. Smoke, words, but with her belly smack in the middle! He's the one who's making her have second thoughts!
PROFESSOR: No.
FRIEND: Oh yes, you can be sure of it. And it makes me sick. He makes me sick, you make me sick!

PROFESSOR: I know he's not interested in being a father. Not interested in the slightest.
FRIEND: You? You know that? You know everything, don't you? And just how do you know?
PROFESSOR: I talked to him.
FRIEND: Aha, you talked to him. You talked to him about this and didn't even have the common decency to tell me about it? You saw me going crazy and said nothing? Don't you see that if what you say is true, everything is changed? I thought. . . But then it will be easy to convince her.
PROFESSOR: I talked to him afterwards. After I left here.
FRIEND: What? You saw him? Now, just a while ago?
PROFESSOR (*Trapped*): Well, yes, a short while ago.
FRIEND: He doesn't want to be a father! And when did you see him? Before or after you were beaten up? Before, of course. But you couldn't have done so much in so little time. *(Suddenly his stance and voice stiffen.)* Hey, who did this to you? You still haven't told me.
PROFESSOR: It doesn't matter. A sexual affair. I'm not going to lower myself to the sordid details.
FRIEND: He did it, didn't he! It was him.
PROFESSOR: No! You don't know what you're talking about!
FRIEND: It was him. Goddam him!
PROFESSOR: I'm telling you it wasn't.
FRIEND: Well then tell me who. Lower yourself to the sordid details, will you? I want to hear the details. I am quite conventional, you know, but I won't blush. Or, aren't there as many sordid details as you might have led me to think: Tell me who beat you up!
PROFESSOR: And so what, if it was him? Maybe it's my fault. (*Pause.*) Okay, it was him. And now what?

(*Pause.*)

FRIEND: He's finished.
PROFESSOR: I'm not going to file charges. Don't even think that.
FRIEND: It doesn't matter. He's finished. For starters I'll have him kicked out of the university. I'll find a way.
PROFESSOR: Because he beat me up or because he got your daughter pregnant? If it's on my account, you can just leave me out. My affairs are mine, not yours, thank you. And besides, that young man. . . You don't understand him. I don't either. In any event, we cannot predict the future. Not you, not I, not anyone.
FRIEND: What are you saying? He is not the future!
PROFESSOR: I would like your grandchild to be born.

FRIEND: No! I look at you, I see you and... What are you becoming? A frightened beast searching for comfort with some threads of cheap metaphysics? An heir who will save you from I-don't-know what future? An angel, right? An angel, isn't that it?

PROFESSOR: That boy and you are so much alike...

FRIEND: You have loved me. I don't know if I am supposed to be happy about that. But if I had to respond to your affection, I can most certainly tell you that... well, I'd like to be brave enough to... I would rather see you dead than turned into some irrational, frightened, pitiful beast.

PROFESSOR *(If he was sitting, now standing up):* You are carrying the burden of Historical Reason with capital letters... Okay, I might tell you that everything has been said. I asked you for two things. One has gotten you very upset. The other, the other... is the disk.

FRIEND: Here.

PROFESSOR: I don't want to fight any more. I'm leaving. I'm tired and you've got to be tired, too. A long day, as they say.

FRIEND: I'm sorry. You upset me. I said some dumb things that I really didn't mean. Come on, I'll take you home.

PROFESSOR: No. I can drive and I have my car here. Besides, if I crash you can thank Divine Providence. I will have died before baring my wounds. The moral ones, I mean.

FRIEND: Very funny. Why is it you need the disk?

PROFESSOR: We'll call each other tomorrow, okay?

(Pause.)

FRIEND: Gerard, I want to help you.

(The PROFESSOR extends his hand and they shake hands like good friends.)

PROFESSOR: We'll call each other tomorrow.

(The PROFESSOR leaves. The FRIEND quietly watches him exit. He then reacts and walks around nervously. He goes to the telephone, looks up a number and dials.)

YOUNG MAN'S VOICE: Hello.

FRIEND: I called you earlier and left a message on your answering machine that I wanted to see you. Did you get the message?

YOUNG MAN'S VOICE: Oh, it's you.

FRIEND: I want to see you. Right away.

YOUNG MAN'S VOICE: We can agree quickly enough on what to do about your daughter. There's no need for us to see each other.
FRIEND: My daughter is not going to be the main topic of the conversation.
YOUNG MAN'S VOICE: I can't leave my place.
FRIEND: I'll come over.
YOUNG MAN'S VOICE: I can't leave here because I'm busy.
FRIEND: Stop fishing for excuses! It's no use, I'm coming over. Do you understand? Right now!

(The sound of another phone call drowns out their voices. As this new conversation goes on for a moment, the FRIEND continues talking to the Young Man, but we cannot hear what they are saying. The lights go down. It is on this darkened stage, then, that an anonymous woman tells her story to another woman.)

VOICE OF THE EXASPERATED WOMAN: He didn't come. He's run away. I thought he was kidding, that they were just words. We had a fight, you know? And he didn't show up after work. I waited for hours, dying of anxiety. That's why I called you. Maybe you... If you see him, tell him not to make me suffer. You don't want him to make me suffer any more, do you? You'll tell him, won't you? Tell him to call me, any way. I don't care at what hour. If only I didn't love him! He's the only one I'd go to bed with, with no one else. How can it be that I love him if I feel so miserable, miserable, miserable... Loving is a disease, that's what it is. If I could only free myself! He must come back, he must, I can't go on. Loving costs so much. I don't want to be alone. Fever and suffering, that's loving. Punishment from heaven, there's no reason why and you can't make any sense out of anything. A disease.
VOICE OF THE CALM WOMAN: A disease that will go away. And it will go away, you'll see.
VOICE OF THE EXASPERATED WOMAN: A disease. It catches up with you and you're lost. The feelings, if they get at your heart, have to be cut off. Before they destroy you. Love is a trick. A disease, the beginning of a disease...

SCENE FIVE

The telephone conversation fades as the lights come back on. We are in the YOUNG MAN's setting. He and the FRIEND are arguing.

FRIEND: My daughter can have sex with whomever she wants. If at one point in time she chose you, too bad. The smart guy who's made it on his own. You've paraded your arrogance all around the university, showing that you're smarter than everyone else and you're unrelenting with both your fellow students and your teachers. I've never liked you. I don't feel sorry for you. That's not what you were interested in, and you've gotten what you wanted. You are unpleasant. And you've gotten my daughter pregnant. You don't love her, do you? Maybe she loves you, I don't know, but she'll get over it.
YOUNG MAN: Yes, she'll get over it.
FRIEND: You're not interested in her, not interested in having children. . . and I'm glad. I did not know that before. But now I do and so we really could have taken care of this over the phone. The problem. . . There's another problem. Do you like medieval literature?
YOUNG MAN: The professor who teaches the seminar is pretty good.
FRIEND (*Harshly*): What happened to him?
YOUNG MAN: You're friends, aren't you? Have you seen him?
FRIEND: You beat him up.
YOUNG MAN: So he told you. I can't blame him. Has he filed charges?
FRIEND: No.
YOUNG MAN: So what's he waiting for? I told him to.
FRIEND: Why the beating?
YOUNG MAN: Whatever he told you is undoubtedly true.
FRIEND: He didn't tell me anything.
YOUNG MAN (*Surprised*): What?
FRIEND: Nothing. He didn't say a word.
YOUNG MAN: Oh. (*Pause.*) Let's respect his silence, shall we?
FRIEND: I want to know what happened! I won't leave until I find out. Just give me one reason for what you did, goddam it! (*Pause, searching for the right words.*) If you feel ashamed. Maybe it's not you who should feel ashamed. Maybe you got angry at him because. . . (*Blurting out.*) Did he make you a proposition?

(*Pause.*)

YOUNG MAN (*Cynically*): What kind of proposition?

FRIEND (*Worried, wondering if the Young Man is aware of the Professor's inclinations*): I don't know. . . Did you have an argument? Something happened! You wouldn't have beaten him up for no reason at all!
YOUNG MAN: If he kept quiet about it, so will I. Drop it, will you?
FRIEND: It doesn't matter if he doesn't file charges. I want to know so I know what to do. You beat up a sick man. A truly heroic feat. You have destroyed a failing man. If his condition worsens because of what you did. . .
YOUNG MAN (*Cutting him off as he realizes what he has been told*): Sick?
FRIEND: Yes, sick.
YOUNG MAN: What do you mean, sick? The flu?
FRIEND: He's dying. We'll see how long he lasts. He doesn't think anyone knows and when he tells you, it's your job to act surprised.
YOUNG MAN: He's dying? He's a good teacher. Shit.
FRIEND: You don't have to tell me about your relationship with my daughter, but I need to know what happened between you and him. Do you understand now?

(The phone rings. The YOUNG MAN hesitates for a moment but picks up the receiver before the answering machine clicks on.)

YOUNG MAN: Hello.
PROFESSOR'S VOICE: I need to see you.
YOUNG MAN: You shouldn't call me. Maybe I was going to call you. (*To the FRIEND.*) It's him.
FRIEND: He's crazy. He still wants you!
YOUNG MAN (*Into the receiver, trying hard to sound nice*): I guess I should apologize, sir.
PROFESSOR'S VOICE: Are you going to call me sir again? Can you come over to my house? I won't keep you long.
YOUNG MAN: Me, in your house, again?
PROFESSOR'S VOICE: Please. I want to finish something. I can't wait.
FRIEND: He wants you to go over to his place? After what you did to him? Has he lost his mind?
YOUNG MAN: I'll call you back in five minutes to tell you if I can or not.
PROFESSOR'S VOICE: Okay.

(THEY hang up.)

YOUNG MAN: Well, you heard him. Maybe I should go now.
FRIEND: Be careful.
YOUNG MAN: I don't need your advice.

FRIEND: Seeing you will do him no good. But, there's nothing I can do about it. . . Remember he's a sick man. Don't make his life impossible.
YOUNG MAN: I'll listen to his. . . What did you call them? His propositions?
FRIEND: What does he want from you? Did he tell you?
YOUNG MAN: No.
FRIEND: Listen to him, and if you don't like what he tells you, just keep it to yourself. No matter what. Just keep it to yourself!
YOUNG MAN: What are you afraid of? Are you afraid I'll beat him up again? Enough is enough! Propositions. Yes, he made "propositions." So don't get all upset. I'm not shocked, I'm not going to lose my composure. Does that satisfy you?
FRIEND: I knew it. That's why you fought. He just kept on insisting and insisting and you lost control.
YOUNG MAN: He didn't insist too much. Not in that sense. You don't have to try to justify my actions. Didn't you say you don't like me? Then don't try to justify me. You haven't understood a thing. *(The phone rings. Pause. The YOUNG MAN picks it up.)* Hello, who is this?
SENSUAL MALE VOICE: I want to see you nude and hold you.
YOUNG MAN *(Smiling, maliciously, turning towards the FRIEND)*: Maybe now you'll see. *(Into the receiver.)* Hi, nice to hear you. Loyal customers like you deserve to be treated nicely. *(Laughing.)* Discount included. Are you sure you want to see me nude and hold me? You can strip me yourself. Or do you want me to open the door naked?
SENSUAL MALE VOICE: Any way you turn me on. When can I come? I'm in a hurry.
YOUNG MAN: Cool down, man. Give me a couple of hours.
SENSUAL MALE VOICE: I don't know if I can stand it. Are you with another customer?
YOUNG MAN: I'm with something that's sort of like a customer, I guess. I can't for the next couple of hours. Call me before to make sure I've gotten home. I have to go out. And think about me, in the meantime. Let your imagination run wild and rev up your engine.

(He hangs up. The FRIEND is shocked.)

FRIEND: You. . .
YOUNG MAN: Yep, I charge for sex. Prostitution. Male. A fucking faggot.
FRIEND: My daughter. . .
YOUNG MAN: I like women too. Don't you get it? And now I'm going to see your friend. My problems with him are none of your business.

(Pause.)

FRIEND: You're through. When I came I was willing to make a deal. I thought I had you figured out, but I guess not well enough. (*Pause.*) I'll make your life impossible for you. I'll make it impossible for you to get into any center of learning. I'll find a way, I swear. So you like studying? Well, good-bye. I have some influence, you know. I'll show everyone you are a no good bastard. Forget my daughter, forget my friend, just go hustling and drown yourself in shit. My only goal in life will be to annihilate you. The only thing you'll be able to do is service them, as long as they find you attractive, and then commit suicide, just like your father.

(Pause. The YOUNG MAN looks as if he is going to explode. But he retains his composure and after a moment of tension, instead of answering, he dials a phone number.)

PROFESSOR'S VOICE: Hello.
YOUNG MAN: I'm coming over.
FRIEND: You're worse than dead. *(He turns around and exits.)*
PROFESSOR'S VOICE: How soon will you get here?
YOUNG MAN: No more than fifteen minutes. I have to be back home in a couple of hours.
PROFESSOR'S VOICE: You will be. I'm glad. I should feel sad, but now...

(The sound of another phone conversation drowns out their voices. As this phone call takes place, the YOUNG MAN keeps on talking to the Professor for a short while at least, without our hearing what they say, and then black out. The anonymous phone call between the voice of an OLD WOMAN and that of a VERY YOUNG BOY takes place with the lights down.)

VOICE OF THE OLD WOMAN: Why are you sad? I know, I'm old and you can't tell me because I wouldn't understand.
VOICE OF THE VERY YOUNG BOY: I like to listen to you. I like to listen to you, Grandma.
VOICE OF THE OLD WOMAN: If I could be next to you... You're so young. You're worried and that's what happens when you're alone and you begin to think about little things and you make mountains out of mole hills. Isn't that it?
VOICE OF THE VERY YOUNG BOY: Probably...
VOICE OF THE OLD WOMAN: Relax. If only I could hold you... But you'll see. Your sadness will fade away in your sleep. Sleep makes worries disappear. I'm telling you, have hope, tomorrow you won't be worried about anything. Tomorrow, you'll see, tomorrow you'll feel fine again. Your worries will have faded away.

SCENE SIX

The phone conversation fades as the lights come up and we are in the PROFESSOR's setting. The PROFESSOR has changed clothes and greets the YOUNG MAN.

YOUNG MAN (*Uncomfortable*): May I ask how you are?
PROFESSOR: Please, don't be so formal.
YOUNG MAN: I can't stay long. A customer is waiting.
PROFESSOR: It was nice of you to come, then.
YOUNG MAN: Are you making fun of me?
PROFESSOR: No.
YOUNG MAN: I don't want you to "pardon" me. I don't expect that and I don't want it. But please forgive me for losing my head and hurting you.
PROFESSOR: Please, relax and treat me like a friend.
YOUNG MAN: I'm sorry I kicked the shit out of you and I'm sorry I broke the computer.
PROFESSOR: I didn't call you to hear you apologize. Just forget it. You didn't like it when I told you you were fond of me. And yet you do feel some fondness for me. You, the man who believes in nothing, much less in affection.
YOUNG MAN (*After a pause*): Perhaps. Maybe I feel a certain. . . How are you? You should see a doctor.
PROFESSOR: It's not your beating that's going to kill me.
YOUNG MAN: You're sick, aren't you?
PROFESSOR: Sick? (*Pause.*) Oh yes, my friend has gone into action. The father of the girl you were ditching.
YOUNG MAN: Yes, he has.
PROFESSOR: He'll make your life impossible. I won't be able to stop him.
YOUNG MAN: It doesn't matter.
PROFESSOR: It'll be tough on you.
YOUNG MAN: It doesn't matter.
PROFESSOR: Yes, I'm sick. And I have a present for you. Wait, it's not money or anything similar. . . Oh, let's just forget it. I went too far in suggesting anything. Let's see. I shall try to be clear and to the point, since you have to leave. The issue is I'm ill and I might not have enough time left to rewrite the essay.
YOUNG MAN: I don't know what to say. I destroyed it.
PROFESSOR: Don't get carried away. Nothing irreparable has happened. At least not yet. You destroyed the disk I gave you and the computer the book was written on. But, there was one other disk. (*HE shows it to him.*) This is it.
YOUNG MAN: I'm glad. I was pretty naïve to believe I destroyed your monograph. Fortunately.

PROFESSOR: Oh, but you still can. Now you can. This disk is all that's left. There are no other copies. And here's my proposal. I don't think we're ever going to see each other again. Even if I try to convince him otherwise, my friend is not going to let you go back to the university.

YOUNG MAN: I know.

PROFESSOR: Classes are over. The seminar on medieval literature is finished. I'm going to miss you.

YOUNG MAN: I'm going to miss going to your class, too.

PROFESSOR: And we won't be seeing each other outside class, either. There's no reason to. We're finished with Lully. The Friend and the Beloved are over.

YOUNG MAN: Well, there's nothing we can do about that.

PROFESSOR: True. At the risk of repeating myself, but since this is the last time, I shall dare to suggest that you have a child some day. You won't listen to me, but that's the suggestion. And then, well, I'll get to the point. I want to give you a present of sorts. And you must accept it. That's why I asked you to come. The disk. I'm giving it to you. A great present, I know. Do whatever you want with it.

YOUNG MAN: No. I won't take it. No.

PROFESSOR: Take it.

YOUNG MAN: No! What am I supposed to do with it? No!

PROFESSOR: It's for you.

YOUNG MAN: It's for your friend, or for somebody else. For whoever's going to edit the book and all that junk! I can't do anything with it. I don't want it. I don't want to take responsibility for it.

PROFESSOR: It is my wish that you have it. Not my friend, not some editor, but you. And do whatever you want to with it.

YOUNG MAN: No way! Where did you get this idea?

PROFESSOR: It's yours. All my hard work, what I love the most, what you don't understand and what my friend doesn't like because it talks about salvation, I want all of those ridiculous ideas in your hands. I give it to you.

YOUNG MAN: Why are you doing this? Why? Is it because you love me? You love me this much?

PROFESSOR: I'd like to think of you as my son.

YOUNG MAN: You don't have a son and I don't have a father! My father was an asshole. A pathetic clown! Fathers, sons, can't you think about anything else? My father! My father was zilch! Zilch! He died the way he was supposed to die! He's forgotten. Do you remember the trash you threw out yesterday? Well, I don't remember my father!

PROFESSOR: You love him. You've always loved him. You feel sad about his death and you feel sad because you have been unable to hold onto his stupid beliefs. His failure, that he wasn't right, hurt you very, very much. You haven't been able to hold on to anything since. He thought he could go forward, in one way or another.

That's it, isn't it? I believe in much less. (*Pause.*) I love you as much as you loved your father. (*Pause.*) The disk is yours.

(The PROFESSOR tosses it and the YOUNG MAN, instinctively, pulls it out of the air. He stares at it as if it were burning his hand.)

YOUNG MAN: You won't trap me! You want to trap me, but you're not going to.

(Pause.)

PROFESSOR: Just imagine. . . that this disk. . . is the legacy from your father.

(Pause. Then, suddenly full of rage, the YOUNG MAN breaks the disk.)

YOUNG MAN (*As if he had escaped from a threatening beast*): Get out of my life! (*The broken disk bounces on the floor. Pause. He looks at the PROFESSOR, who has hardly shown any emotion. Softly.*) You asked for this. (*Louder.*) You asked for this! I didn't! You made me do this! You made me! Go to hell! Asshole! You made me!

PROFESSOR (*Calmly*): Calm down. You can't do anything now. And it was yours. You could do whatever you wanted to with it. You have to accept what happened. You'll have to learn how to accept it.

YOUNG MAN: I can't!

PROFESSOR: You'll have to. You're trapped. You see? Now you're trapped.

YOUNG MAN: Trapped?

PROFESSOR: You read the essay. You're the only person who did. When I die there will only be odd fragments in your memory. The essay is truly yours. And only yours. A legacy. You may use it or not, but it is an inheritance you cannot refuse. It's a part of you.

YOUNG MAN: I can't remember anything.

PROFESSOR: Are you sure?

YOUNG MAN: You son of a bitch.

PROFESSOR: I gave you what I had to give you.

YOUNG MAN: Did you get me mad just so I would destroy it?

PROFESSOR: No. I took that chance. I wasn't sure. But that's the way it happened. My only heir. I'm not unhappy.

YOUNG MAN: Nothing will happen. Nothing will change.

PROFESSOR: I won't live long enough to follow your life. I hope it's long, I really do. And you won't be able to explain it to me because you don't know how things are going to go. Too bad. I would have liked that, but (*Pause.*) I'm not unhappy. (*Pause. His tone becomes lighter.*) You know you're late. You have to go.

YOUNG MAN: I know.
PROFESSOR: Good-bye. (*The YOUNG MAN doesn't move.*) You're leaving with what you came for. Good-bye. What else are you waiting for?
YOUNG MAN: Nothing else.

(*The YOUNG MAN turns around and leaves. The PROFESSOR is alone.*)

PROFESSOR: I am not unhappy. (*Pause. The phone rings. He picks it up.*) Hello.
FRIEND'S VOICE: Is that idiot there?
PROFESSOR (*Laughing*): He just left.
FRIEND'S VOICE: I'll make him pay! Did you get rid of him? How are you?
PROFESSOR: Fine.
FRIEND'S VOICE: I don't believe you.
PROFESSOR: Better than you think.
FRIEND'S VOICE: No odd pain? If you need me. . .
PROFESSOR: I don't need anything.
FRIEND'S VOICE: But if you do need something, tell me. No matter what time it is.
PROFESSOR: I just need rest. Just some rest. And that's what I'm going to do. I know I'll be able to rest.

(*The sound of another phone conversation drowns out this conversation. As this phone call takes place, the PROFESSOR keeps on talking to the FRIEND for a short while at least, without our hearing what they say, and then the lights go out. The anonymous phone call between TWO WOMEN takes place with the lights out.*)

1ST WOMAN'S VOICE: You'll try to rest, you'll try to relax. . . ? That's easy to say. You won't be able to, you know?
2ND WOMAN'S VOICE: Calm down, calm down. Nothing's the matter. A good sense of humor and I'll manage.
1ST WOMAN'S VOICE: You don't seem to have heard me. Don't you realize what's going on?
2ND WOMAN'S VOICE: Nothing is going on. If you were me, you'd say nothing. Little everyday things can bring nice things that can make us so happy. . . the little things are enough to give you something almost like happiness.
1ST WOMAN'S VOICE: You don't want to know.
2ND WOMAN'S VOICE: Maybe not. But I know what awaits me today. The same as everyday. And what do you want me to say? I don't need anything else. Really. I don't need to go any deeper. That's what I think happiness is. And it's mine. I don't expect anything else. I've already got happiness.

SCENE SEVEN

The phone conversation fades. In the meantime the lights come up and we are in the YOUNG MAN'S setting. HE enters just now, absorbed in his thoughts. HE glances at the answering machine and sees there is a message. HE turns it on.

YOUNG WOMAN'S VOICE: You're not home? I haven't been in touch because my mother was here being a pain. My parents will take care of the medical bills and everything. (*Pause.*) I don't know. I still don't know. And if I don't have an abortion? A spark of life. . . You wouldn't understand. A spark of myself. Don't worry, I don't need you. The child, if there is one, won't be your concern. (*Pause.*) If you feel like it, call me, and if you don't, drop dead.

(The message ends. The YOUNG MAN is thinking. HE walks around and maybe takes his jacket off. HE looks at the phone from a certain distance. HE makes up his mind and approaches the phone. But at that moment the phone rings. A shrug of disgust, and HE picks up the phone.)

YOUNG MAN: Hello.
SENSUAL MALE VOICE: You're home.
YOUNG MAN: Yeah. Come on over. I'm waiting.
SENSUAL MALE VOICE: I'll be there right away. I'm in a bar nearby. I couldn't wait any longer.
YOUNG MAN (*Laughing*): You are impatient.
SENSUAL MALE VOICE: Something like that.
YOUNG MAN: You're up for lots of excitement, huh?
SENSUAL MALE VOICE: This time I want you all to myself the whole night.
YOUNG MAN: Never say no to a good customer.
SENSUAL MALE VOICE: Let your imagination go, and the cash will flow.
YOUNG MAN: We'll get it on. You know, that's why you come back.
SENSUAL MALE VOICE: Yes, that's why I always come back for more.
YOUNG MAN: And it won't be the last time.
SENSUAL MALE VOICE: That depends on you.
YOUNG MAN: You'll come back. You'll have no choice. It'll be the fuck of your life. And you'll come back again and again. No one can give you what I can. I like you. And I need the cash. (*Pause. Half-laughing.*) Hell, I have a kid to support.

(The sound of two consecutive phone conversations drowns out their voices. After a moment, the YOUNG MAN hangs up. We hear the first conversation as he slowly begins to undress.)

1ST MALE VOICE: Life is painful. We try to get rid of our pain and the only thing we achieve is passing it on to others.
2ND MALE VOICE: Words! Excuses! You're a real bastard!
1ST MALE VOICE: I am not. And you aren't, either. It's what happened, so what do you want? Surges of pain reach us, one after another, and we never cease to send our own waves of pain to others. You're wrong if you think I won. The worst part of pain is that no one wins, it's no good for anything.
2ND MALE VOICE: Will you shut up? I'll make you pay for this! I'm not going to forget this, and don't play word games with me! You'll pay for this! You get it? Huh? You're going to pay for this!

(The YOUNG MAN has taken all his clothes off, piece by piece. Meanwhile, the second phone conversation ties in with the earlier one.)

FEMALE VOICE: Calm down. Just accept it, don't get upset!
3RD MALE VOICE: Accept what? Accept, resign myself, never, do you understand? None of you knows me! I will not resign myself to this. You think I'm through, you feel sorry for me, and with a bit of luck you'll feel mercy for my meaningless failure!
FEMALE VOICE: No! We love you! No!
3RD MALE VOICE: Oh, yes, in your own way maybe you're right. But listen, I'm not going to let it go at this. I will not take this sitting down!

(Now completely nude, the YOUNG MAN puts on one of his possible professional uniforms: something strident, obscene, vulgar but probably effective. It doesn't hide his nudity but rather adds to it and accentuates it.)

3RD MALE VOICE: This isn't the end, don't get me wrong, I'm not dead, I still have time! And I couldn't give a shit about your righteous sympathy! I'll get there, do you understand? Yes, I'll get there! Against all of you, I'll finally reach my goal. One day I will. One day.....some day I'll find what I'm looking for, and then the time will come when your laughter will freeze, that day will come and I will have saved myself! I will have invented salvation! I will have invented salvation! I will have invented salvation!

(Suddenly, abruptly, the apartment doorbell sounds loudly. The telephone voices stop at once. Total silence. Pause. The YOUNG MAN is ready. HE looks at the door.)

BLACK OUT

CRITICAL REACTION TO THE PLAY

Psychology, not politics, was a more frequent focus of. . . *Testament* [*Legacy*]. In Sergi Belbel's uninhibited staging, three well-known television actors dove headlong into Jornet's sordid themes--male prostitution, abortion, sado-masochism--and swept the audience enthusiastically along. A first-night performance in the neoclassical Teatro Romea. . . was greeted with cheers and repeated curtain calls.

Jim O'Quinn
American Theatre (January 1998)

The talented author sets up a game of short, harsh situations. Gradually the three characters, aided by the stifling presence of the telephone, begin to change. In a dramatically effective way, ideology is rapidly overwhelmed by and converted into life.

Lorenzo López Sancho
ABC (Madrid, March 1996)

Starting from love, fear, and some people's obsession with perpetuating their ideas, the play speaks of moral and intellectual heritage. The author pushes the characters toward moral courage, an option that is not easy in the disconcerting, fearful times in which we live.

Gonzalo Pérez de Olaguer
El Periódico (Barcelona, July 1997)

In *Legacy* the playwright gives forceful expression to generational conflict. He reveals the bankruptcy of dialogue between old idealists and fiercely pragmatic youth. Finally, in this story that serves as a mirror of society, he illuminates the converging shadows by voting in favor of hope.. . . . The first encounters of the professor with his student and with his old college friend are two of the best scenes to be found in our contemporary theatre.

Joan-Anton Benach
La Vanguardia (Barcelona, Dec. 1997)

I realize that I have reduced Benet's play to the relationship between professor and student, between father and son, because that is what affects me most. What moves me in Benet's play is this effort to safeguard and perpetuate one's memory.

Joan de Sagarra
El País (Madrid, July 1997)

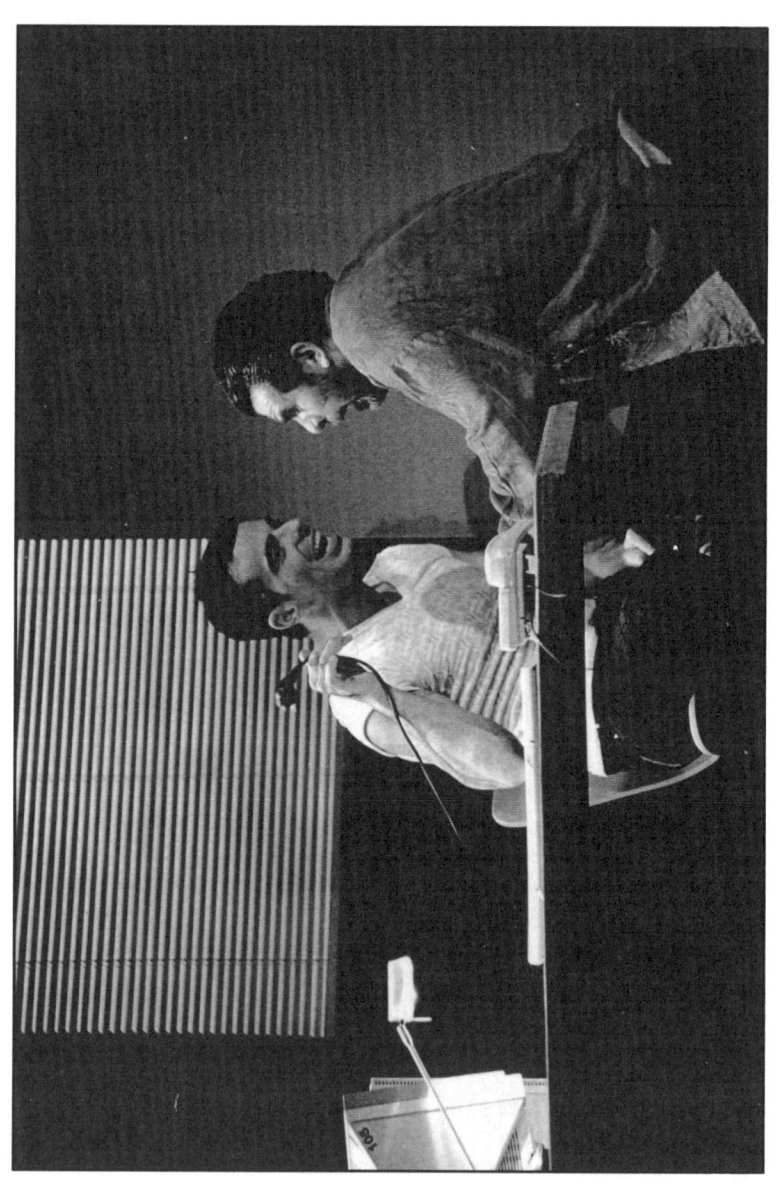

Legacy in Barcelona, 1997. Photo by Pilar Aymerich.

TRANSLATOR'S ACKNOWLEDGMENTS

I was very pleased when my friend and former colleague Phyllis Zatlin asked me if I would be interested in translating *Testament* into English. Several people have helped to improve my initial draft; I would especially like to thank Marion P. Holt, Lorenzo Mans, and Len Mazzarra for their very careful reading of the text and Eulàlia Borràs for her note on the author. Margrette Brown helped with the final preparation of the edition. I am most grateful to Phyllis Zatlin, who was not only willing to include a play in this series that was originally written in Catalan, but also ready to edit it. Any translator would appreciate the time and effort she has spent on seeing this project through, and I take this opportunity to thank her.

A grant from the Institució de les Lletres Catalanes, Conselleria de Cultura of the Generalitat de Catalunya is gratefully acknowledged.

ABOUT THE TRANSLATOR

Janet DeCesaris first became interested in translation while a student at Georgetown University, where she earned a B. S. in Language in 1977. She then went on to graduate studies in linguistics and Spanish at Indiana University (Ph.D., 1988), and learned Catalan while an exchange student at the University of Barcelona. She taught in the Department of Spanish and Portuguese at Rutgers, The State University of New Jersey for three years before settling permanently in the Barcelona metropolitan area. She is the co-author (with Patricia V. Lunn) of an advanced level textbook on Spanish grammar (*Investigación de gramática*, 1992). She has taught Catalan linguistics at the University of Barcelona, Rovira i Virgili University in Tarragona, and currently teaches translation, English, and linguistics at Pompeu Fabra University in Barcelona. She is an active member of the University's research group in applied linguistics, and recently has translated into English the Official Guide to Montserrat (1998) and the textbook *Terminology* by Teresa Cabré (1999).

ENTRE ACTOS: DIÁLOGOS SOBRE TEATRO ESPAÑOL ENTRE SIGLOS

MARTHA T. HALSEY y PHYLLIS ZATLIN, editores

42 ensayos sobre teatro español contemporáneo

Reflexionan sobre su propio teatro Luis Araújo, Josep M. Benet i Jornet, Jerónimo López Mózo, Paloma Pedrero y José María Rodríguez Méndez.

37 estudios sobre el teatro de Rafael Alberti, Max Aub, Antonio Buero Vallejo, Ernesto Caballero, Joaquín Calvo Sotelo, Ana Diosdado, Antonio Gala, Luis Miguel González Cruz, Maribel Lázaro, Federico García Lorca, Jorge Márquez, Manuel Martínez Mediero, Ignacio del Moral, Lauro Olmo, Paloma Pedrero, Pilar Pombo, José María Rodríguez Méndez, Concha Romero, Víctor Ruiz Iriarte, José Sanchis Sinisterra, y Alfonso Sastre así como estudios panorámicos sobre el teatro vanguardista y posmoderno en España y sobre la dramaturgia femenina en los 90.
(24 trabajos en español y 18 en inglés) 405 pp.

$26.50 U.S. (porte pagado)

PEDIDOS A:
    ESTRENO: ESTUDIOS
    352 N. Burrowes Bldg.
    Penn State University
    University Park, PA 16802 U.S.A.

ESTRENO:
CUADERNOS DEL TEATRO
ESPANOL CONTEMPORANEO

Published at Ohio Wesleyan University
Sandra Harper, Ed.
Phyllis Zatlin, Assoc. Ed.

A journal featuring play texts of previously unpublished works from contemporary Spain, interviews with playwrights, directors, and critics, and extensive critical studies in both Spanish and English.

Plays published have included texts by Buero-Vallejo, Sastre, Arrabal, Gala, Nieva, Salom, Martín Recuerda, Olmo, Martínez Mediero, F. Cabal, P. Pedrero and Onetti. The journal carries numerous photographs of recent play performances in Spain and elsewhere, including performances in translation.

Also featured are an annual bibliography, regular book reviews, and critiques of the recent theater season, as well as a round table in which readers from both the U. S. and Spain share information and engage in lively debates.

ESTRENO also publishes a series of translations of contemporary Spanish plays which may be subscribed to separately.

Orders to: *ESTRENO*
203A University Hall
61 South Sandusky Street
Ohio Wesleyan University
Delaware, Ohio 43015
USA

Individual subscriptions are $15.00 and institutional subscriptions, $28.00 for the calendar year.

ESTRENO Plays is a series of stageworthy translations including works by J. L. Alonso de Santos, Luis Araújo, Fernando Arrabal, J. M. Benet i Jornet, Antonio Buero-Vallejo, Fermín Cabal, Ana Diosdado, Pilar Enciso, Antonio Gala, José López Rubio, M. Martínez Mediero, Lauro Olmo, Paloma Pedrero, Jaime Salom, Alfonso Sastre, Ramón del Valle-Inclán, Alfonso Vallejo, and other autors.

List price, nos. 1-11: $6; nos. 12-20 & rev. 6, $8; 40% discount to bookstores and dealers.

Visit our web page at www.rci.rutgers.edu/~estrplay/webpage.html
or request our catalog by contacting:

Estreno Plays, Department of Spanish & Portuguese
Rutgers, The State University of New Jersey
105 George Street
New Brunswick, NJ 08901-1414
FAX: 732/932-9837   Phone: 732/932-9412x25
E-mail: estrplay@rci.rutgers.edu

Special offer: 3 or more volumes, $5 each. Mention this ad at time of order.